LEADING
RESIDENTIAL
ARCHITECTS

ALLEN-CHERRY DESIGN-BUILD • AM JOHNSON ARCHITECTS • ARCHITECTONICS • AVANT

ARCHITECTS • BLUE SKY STUDIO • BOULER DESIGN GROUP • BRIGGS ARCHITECTURE + DESIGN

BURGE & ASSOCIATES ARCHITECTS • CHERI BELZ, ARCHITECT • CHRISTOPHER ROSE ARCHITECTS • DAWSON

MISSMACH ARCHITECTS • DOMINICK TRINGALI ARCHITECTS • DUBBE-MOULDER ARCHITECTS • HARRIS &

ASSOCIATES ARCHITECTS   J. GRAHAM GOLDSMITH

ARCHITECTS • JAFFA   GROUP • JEFFREY L.

MILLER ARCHITECT • JOHN MORRIS ARCHITECTS • KEN TATE ARCHITECT • LEVIN/BROWN & ASSOCIATES

LOONEY RICKS KISS ARCHITECTS • MCLAUGHLIN & ASSOCIATES ARCHITECTS • PARKER & ASSOCIATES ARCHITECTS

ROB BRAMHALL ARCHITECTS • ROBINETTE ARCHITECTS • SHAMBURGER DESIGN STUDIO • THE LYONS

DESIGN GROUP • THOMAS BAIO ARCHITECT • VANGUARD STUDIO • WELLS + ASSOCIATES ARCHITECTS

DESIGN GROUP ■ THOMAS BAIO ARCHITECT ■ VANGUARD STUDIO ■ WELLS + ASSOCIATES ARCHITECTS

ROB BRAMHALL ARCHITECTS ■ ROBINETTE ARCHITECTS ■ SHAMBURGER DESIGN STUDIO ■ THE LYONS

LOONEY RICKS KISS ARCHITECTS ■ MCLAUGHLIN & ASSOCIATES ARCHITECTS ■ PARKER & ASSOCIATES ARCHITECTS

MILLER ARCHITECT ■ JOHN MORRIS ARCHITECTS ■ KEN TATE ARCHITECT ■ LEVIN/BROWN & ASSOCIATES

ARCHITECTS ■ JAFFA GROUP ■ JEFFREY L.

ASSOCIATES ARCHITECTS J. GRAHAM GOLDSMITH

WISSMACH ARCHITECTS ■ DOMINICK TRINGALI ARCHITECTS ■ DUBBE-MOULDER ARCHITECTS ■ HARRIS &

BURDGE & ASSOCIATES ARCHITECTS ■ CHERI BELZ, ARCHITECT ■ CHRISTOPHER ROSE ARCHITECTS ■ DAWSON

ARCHITECTS ■ BLUE SKY STUDIO ■ BOULER DESIGN GROUP ■ BRIGGS ARCHITECTURE + DESIGN

ALLEN-GUERRA DESIGN-BUILD ■ AM JOHNSON ARCHITECTS ■ ARCHITECTONICS ■ AVANT

LEADING RESIDENTIAL ARCHITECTS

A home is more than a matter of five bedrooms, six baths and his-and-her closets. A house can—and should—be a work of art, one in which the proportions and rhythms of daily life come into play, along with aesthetics and craft. It is one thing to quantify what goes into a house (the square footage, ceiling heights, number of rooms) and another to make it a place for the human psyche and human soul. An architect can do just that.

THE PERFECT
HOME

TABLE OF CONTENTS

16	Harris & Associates Architects	Alabama
24	Blue Sky Studio	Alaska
30	Robinette Architects	Arizona
38	Parker & Associates Architects	Arkansas
44	Burdge & Associates Architects	California
52	Allen-Guerra Design-Build	Breckenridge, Colorado
58	Cheri Belz, Architect	Boulder, Colorado
64	AM Johnson Architects	Florida
72	Dawson Wissmach Architects	Georgia
80	McLaughlin & Associates Architects	Idaho
88	The Lyons Design Group	Illinois
94	Wells + Associates Architects	Iowa
100	Ken Tate Architect	Louisiana
108	John Morris Architects	Maine
116	Levin/Brown & Associates	Maryland
122	Rob Bramhall Architects	Massachusetts

TABLE OF CONTENTS

128	Dominick Tringali Architects	Michigan
136	Briggs Architecture + Design	Montana
142	Avant Architects	Nebraska
148	Thomas Baio Architect	New Jersey
154	Bouler Design Group	New York
162	Shamburger Design Studio	North Carolina
170	Jeffrey L. Miller Architect	Oregon
176	Christopher Rose Architects	South Carolina
184	Looney Ricks Kiss Architects	Tennessee
190	Vanguard Studio	Texas
198	Jaffa Group	Utah
206	J. Graham Goldsmith Architects	Vermont
212	Architectonics	Washington
220	Dubbe-Moulder Architects	Wyoming

PRODUCED AND PUBLISHED BY SANDOW MEDIA CORPORATION

All rights reserved. No portion of this book may be reproduced—mechanically, electronically, or by any other means, including photocopying—without written permission from the publisher, except for brief passages that may be quoted for reviews.

The Perfect Home Leading Residential Architects™ is a registered trademark of Sandow Media Corporation. ©2007 All rights reserved.

Library of Congress Catalog Card Number: 2007942200

ISBN: 978-0-9800398-0-1

First Printing: December 2007

10 9 8 7 6 5 4 3 2 1

Printed in China

www.sandowmedia.com

FRONT COVER: Christopher Rose Architects

VICE PRESIDENT CREATIVE DIRECTOR	Yolanda E. Yoh
MANAGING EDITOR	Pamela Lerner Jaccarino
SENIOR PRODUCTION DESIGNER	Svetlana Golub
CONTRIBUTING EDITORS AND WRITERS	Brielle Ferreira, H. Susan Mann, Emily Alice Sacks
DIRECTOR OF CLIENT SERVICES	Tanya Suber
CLIENT SERVICES COORDINATOR	Jamie Beauparlant

Sandow Media Corporation is a cutting-edge media and publishing company built around a single philosophy: always exceed expectations. Based in South Florida, Sandow Media Corporation is defined by an unrelenting drive toward quality and innovation. Founded in 2002 by Adam I. Sandow, Sandow Media specializes in developing distinguished consumer books and magazines in the categories of travel, shelter and beauty. Sandow Media builds uniquely positioned publications that thrive both in print and online. Creativity is at the core of every segment of its business, which is clearly evident in all its products and brands.

SANDOW MEDIA™
Always Exceeding Expectations

CORPORATE HEADQUARTERS
3731 NW 8TH AVENUE
BOCA RATON, FLORIDA 33431
TELEPHONE 561.750.0151 FAX 561.750.0152
www.sandowmedia.com

PRESIDENT AND CHIEF EXECUTIVE OFFICER	Adam I. Sandow
CHIEF OPERATING OFFICER AND CHIEF FINANCIAL OFFICER	Scott R. Yablon
VICE PRESIDENT EDITORIAL AND CREATIVE DIRECTOR	Yolanda E. Yoh
CHIEF SALES OFFICER AND EXECUTIVE VICE PRESIDENT	Erik I. Herz
VICE PRESIDENT OF SALES AND GROUP PUBLISHER	Michael J. Ruskin
VICE PRESIDENT OF REGIONAL SALES, NEWBEAUTY	Steffanie Attenberg
VICE PRESIDENT OF OPERATIONS	Lloyd E. Gilick
MANAGING EDITOR	Pamela Lerner Jaccarino
LUXE ARIZONA – PUBLISHER	Kelly Persellin
LUXE CALIFORNIA – ASSOCIATE PUBLISHER	Cynthia Lapporte
LUXE CHICAGO – ASSOCIATE PUBLISHER	Lisa Fraiberg
LUXE COLORADO – PUBLISHER	Dana L. Meacham
LUXE TEXAS – ASSOCIATE PUBLISHER	Joseph M. Lattimer
CONTROLLER	Larry Edelson-Kayne

Everyone imagines a house at one time or another—from the first stacking of childhood wooden blocks to the elaborate imaginings of pencil on paper. Houses, beautiful houses, are the stuff that dreams are made of. In this book, those dreams become realities with examples of fine architecture across the country, the best works of architects carefully culled to show what a difference design makes.

The houses here come from architects whose work represents various regions of the United States. They do not offer a singular point of view but instead embody a range of architectural thinking. Most of the houses invoke the past in some way—be it the distant past of the Italian Renaissance or the antebellum American South, or a more recent past of the Midwest-bred Prairie School of architecture or the early Modernist period. Some of the houses sprawl through countryside settings, while others fit neatly into urban lots. Most of them are distinctly regional—the New England houses invoking the American Shingle Style, the Western houses echoing the Craftsman tradition.

We are not a nation self-conscious about our history, yet architectural traditions abound here—east and west, north and south. Too often we dismiss our historic architecture as "borrowed" from the English, French, Italian and more, but that is really not the case. There is a rich legacy to draw from, with houses lavish and modest alike. The houses in this book are new, but they celebrate the panorama of our history, interpreting and adapting it as needed. These are houses—be they large or small, brick or wood, stucco or stone—that reflect this rich history but do so in a way that meets modern needs and contemporary lives. Our houses are the building blocks of society. They are the expressions of our hopes and dreams and aspirations. They are an expression of a common aesthetic and of the premium we place—at least some of the time, and one would wish more—on architectural beauty. Houses build neighborhoods, and neighborhoods build communities. Communities, in turn, build societies. It is no exaggeration to say that every house bears that burden or, to put it more optimistically, can embrace that opportunity. That is the mandate at the largest scale.

The German poet Johann Wolfgang von Goethe once said that architecture is "frozen music," and that phrase resonates still. To carry the literary metaphor further, our houses are the instruments to make such music. Each has a solo role and a mission much greater in the larger scheme. Separately, they can be art; together, they can be masterpieces. That is culture. But if houses are culture, they are also comfort. They shelter us, nurture us, offering us a retreat from the rigors of daily life, and keep us safe from harm. Our houses are intensely personal in that they articulate our aspirations and hold our memories. At this level, they are intimate expressions of our identity, and thus we place a premium on them. Some of the ways in which houses express this can be obvious, but there are other ways that are subtler, as repositories of family traditions, as keepers of memories.

Of course, there's function to consider. Obviously, we want our houses to be useful—and usable—but there is more. Houses at their best show us (as individuals, families, a society) at our best. Houses are art, and they are craft.

"Machinery, materials and men—yes—these are the stuffs by means of which the so-called American architect will get his architecture," wrote the greatest of all American architects, Frank Lloyd Wright. "Only by the strength of his spirit's grasp upon all three—machinery, materials and men—will the architect be able so to build that his work may be worthy of the great name architecture."

Trace the house back through history and you will encounter the writings of the first-century BC Roman architect Marcus Vitruvius Pollio, whose words have motivated generations of architects to understand the past and seek out the best, and it is a work that stands today more than two thousand years later. Vitruvius exhorted us to follow the "first principles" of architecture—most often translated as "firmness, commodity and delight." Those principles hold true today when we think about houses: We want them to sit solidly on the ground, and have a substance to them and a capacity to thrill us in ways that are both obvious and subtle.

The history of the Western world is marked by storied architecture—castles, palaces, villas and chateaux that even today evoke our greatest awe and admiration. Elsewhere, Mughal monarchs and Byzantine emperors, among others, were building in styles less familiar but no less breathtaking; the history of the great house is in no way a narrative that takes place only in the Western world. Yet in this "new world," at least in the earliest years of American history, our houses were seldom so formidable. The first settlers who came to Massachusetts and Virginia, and later to other places in the mid-Atlantic and New England seacoasts, found harsh conditions, thus their houses were kept simple; they were modest dwelling places of clapboard or occasionally stone. There are exceptions of course. By the early nineteenth century, there were the antebellum mansions of the South, followed by the great houses of the Hudson River Valley, among others. But Americans tended to live modestly in the early years of this land. "Yet, European splendor was still tempting to many Americans," says Gwendolyn Wright, professor of architecture at Columbia University's Graduate School of Architecture. Wright notes that by the early 1800s, there were a few examples of "stately residential architecture on a scale of size and grandeur found along the avenues of London or Paris."

Today, those models of early architectural splendor are icons of American luxury—museums and historic sites to marvel at. We seek them out, traveling the Natchez Trace or Louisiana's low country to see plantations, or visiting the houses of our early presidents and patriots—George Washington's Mount Vernon, Thomas Jefferson's Monticello, James Madison's Montpelier. We tour the Berkshires and Newport to see the summerhouses of the Gilded Age, homes of the robber barons, the industrial elite, and much more. We drive the streets of tree-shaded suburbs—Shaker Heights, Ohio, or Lake Forest, Illinois—or peer behind the hedgerows in Palm Beach or Southampton to glimpse the grand houses there.

By the latter half of the nineteenth century, Americans were building in earnest, establishing architectural traditions that were very much our own and today much admired—from the Shingle Style to Spanish Colonial Revival (ours, yes, and like

the Florida rendition which we call Mediterranean Revival, ultimately quite American) to the low-slung modern houses of the Prairie School and beyond. The literature recording our architecture—from professional journals to books to women's magazines and newspapers—show us the country's growing fascination with domestic architecture and the burgeoning debates over form and style, design and decoration.

The array of houses on display in this book ranges in size from modest to grand. The houses are linked by the diligence of their designs and the felicity of their execution. We live in a time of enormous growth and expansion—though it varies year by year, the housing stock grows by at least a million new residences annually—and in a time where we build fast and furiously. Today, one can buy and download a house plan (even for a multimillion-dollar mansion) from the Internet, or snatch up the blueprints for a replica of Monticello. In many places and cases, one can create a house the way children make Mr. Potato Head—an arch here, a vault there, a pediment up top and Palladian windows all around. All this makes the work shown in The Perfect Home series of books ever more crucial, ever more notable.

Architecture is both art and craft. A good house requires an understanding of scale and proportion, of construction and detail. A good house may be simplicity itself or it may be elaborate. But behind its design is a breadth of knowledge, a quest for perfection that comes out of the education of our architects.

Why use the services of an architect? Because an architect has the education, training and experience to artistically interpret what a client desires. An architect collaborates and orchestrates the building of a home from concept to reality, bringing flair, imagination, style and value.

A home is more than a matter of five bedrooms, six baths and his-and-her closets. A house can—and should—be a work of art, one in which the proportions and rhythms of daily life come into play, along with aesthetics and craft. It is one thing to quantify what goes into a house (the square footage, ceiling heights, number of rooms) and another to make it a place for the human psyche and human soul. An architect can do just that.

Beth Dunlop

HARRIS & ASSOCIATES ARCHITECTS

alabama

Since its inception in 1987, Harris & Associates continues to establish itself as a force in developing quality designs for residential, commercial and educational purposes. An advocate of no specific architectural style, principal Ray Harris seeks a holistic approach to architecture, creating designs that are responsive to both the environment and his clients' specific needs. Every undertaking is unique to the particular site and the personalities and lifestyles exhibited by the clients, relying on Harris' celebrated blend of practicality and imagination to deliver a truly distinctive project. "Without creativity and artistry, there is no true architecture, only copies of what has been done," Harris says. "An appreciation of what is, with a vision of what can be, is the heart of architecture." With this philosophy at its center, the team at Harris & Associates works collaboratively with their clients to fulfill their dreams and exceed their expectations.

Expansive windows and dramatic lighting invite a visceral reaction to the refined contours of a striking home.

DRAMATIC DESIGN

COMFORT FOOD — *Granite countertops and hardwood floors in basic tones define the kitchen with naturalistic beauty.*

HARRIS & ASSOCIATES ARCHITECTS

ARCHITECTURAL INTEREST ABOUNDS IN THE THEATRICAL LINES OF THE BARREL-VAULTED CEILING AND ARCHED WINDOW.

HARRIS & ASSOCIATES ARCHITECTS

FLOOR-TO-CEILING WINDOWS CAPITALIZE ON SUNLIGHT AND PANORAMIC LAKESIDE VIEWS.

NATURAL STONE, IN A VARIETY OF EARTHY HUES, ESTABLISHES THE FIREPLACE AS THE FOCAL POINT OF THE ROOM.

A wide porch demarks a subtle façade, adorned with windows and glass doors.

PERFECT PORCH

BRICK EMBELLISHMENT *The brick exterior of a traditional residence borrows poise and polish from a classic portico.*

HARRIS & ASSOCIATES ARCHITECTS

A DEN ENCASED IN AFRICAN MAHOGANY CREATES AN INTIMATE SPACE FOR RETREAT AND REPOSE.

BEAUTIFUL BEVELED-GLASS WINDOWS MAINTAIN PRIVACY WHILE ALLOWING LIGHT TO FLOOD IN.

BLUE SKY STUDIO

alaska

Alaska's natural beauty is astounding and severe. Maintaining a balance between a connection to that beauty and a sense of interior warmth is a key element to the talented team at Blue Sky Studio. The firm's enchanting dwellings, constructed with careful consideration to scale, follow the mantra that bigger is not necessarily better, especially in chill-inducing Alaska winters. Careful attention to location, view and daylight creates homes tailored to their sites like fine suits. And while sensible solutions are paramount, aesthetic excellence is never compromised. Blue Sky's projects embrace a variety of genres, from modern to traditional, catering to what each individual client perceives as beautiful. With an open design vision and unfaltering imagination, the firm is continually evolving, generating finished products that are fresh and diverse.

This modern abode is characterized by its sharp angles, neutral palette and unique mixture of textures. **MODERN MASTERPIECE**

DESIGN SQUARED *A simple abode impresses with crisp geometry, transparent layering and indulgent, indigenous landscaping.*

BLUE SKY STUDIO

FLOOR-TO-CEILING WINDOWS INVITE THE OUTSIDE IN;
A ZEBRA CHAIR ADDS A TOUCH OF WHIMSY.

NATURAL WOOD AND STONE FINISHES, CLERESTORY WINDOWS AND
STAINLESS ACCENTS ENHANCE A STREAMLINED KITCHEN.

BLUE SKY STUDIO

THE SKEWED GEOMETRY OF THE FIREPLACE ADDS DRAMA TO THE RECTANGULAR ROOM.

THE CLEAN, SLEEK LINES AND OPEN PLAN MAKE THE KITCHEN IDEAL FOR ENTERTAINING.

No matter how biting the weather, the sweet details and gentle lighting in this cozy bungalow signal warmth. **SWEET SUCCESS**

ROBINETTE ARCHITECTS

arizona

Even though Ron Robinette's work is primarily located in the southwestern environment of Arizona, it captures many styles, from contemporary to Old World traditional. Thoughtfully designed and well detailed, the houses that the firm creates are often winter homes for part-time residents drawn to the beauty of the Sonoran desert landscape. Accordingly, Robinette places a premium on responding to the demands of desert conditions, and designs homes that seem to rise right up from the Southwest's sandy soil. Materials of concrete or masonry, plaster and copper not only beautify the structure, but help protect it from extreme desert climates. Much attention is paid to exterior living spaces and the expansion of interior spaces into the outdoors for year-round use. Quality of construction, sculptural design and the harmony of living both indoors and outdoors are hallmarks of the firm's work. Robinette's hands-on approach, working with clients from start to finish, fosters strong bonds that often turn into lifelong friendships. It's not unusual for Robinette to be asked to create plans for his clients' children, crafting a second generation of homes.

The U-shaped dwelling's inner arch, covered from end to end with floor-to-ceiling windows, encompasses and embraces the beauty of the naturalistic landscaping.

EMBRACING BEAUTY

SLICK BEND — *A structure's delicate curvature provides a smooth contrast to the rugged mountains on the horizon.*

ROBINETTE ARCHITECTS

TEXTURAL SALUTATIONS DRAW VISITORS INDOORS WITH ARTISTIC LIGHT AND ATTENTION TO DETAIL.

ROBINETTE ARCHITECTS

STRONG, WOODEN CEILING BEAMS PROMOTE ARCHITECTURAL INTEREST AND INTEGRITY.

THE SOOTHING, NEUTRAL PALETTE OF A MOUNTAINSIDE RETREAT SUITS ITS SURROUNDINGS.

Fine, antique furnishings reflect the artisan quality of the belabored, tile mosaic underfoot. **CUNNING CRAFT**

ROBINETTE ARCHITECTS

A DRAMATIC WATER FEATURE UNITES CONTEMPORARY INDOOR AND OUTDOOR ELEMENTS.

A CLEVERLY POSITIONED FIREPLACE WARMS GUESTS AT THE ENTRANCE, HERALDING INDOOR COZINESS.

FLOOR-TO-CEILING WINDOWS OFFER ENCHANTING VIEWS OF A WELL-MANICURED BACKYARD.

WITH MOUNTAINS ABOVE AND WATER BELOW, THIS UNASSUMING ABODE FILLS ITS NICHE NICELY.

PARKER & ASSOCIATES ARCHITECTS

arkansas

When Terry Parker founded Parker & Associates Architects in 1994, he brought a wealth of experience and a keen appreciation of architectural excellence to Fayetteville, Arkansas. He also brought a desire to reinterpret and extend the language of residential design. "Traditional architecture is an area of practice that is largely misunderstood and neglected," Parker says. With 26 years of intensive study and construction experience, Parker is well qualified to challenge the boundaries and limitations of traditional residential architecture. He consults with his clients to infuse aspects of their individual personalities into each project he tackles, from small renovations to large custom homes. "We strive to develop an interactive relationship with all of our clients, and we feel that this results in projects that are personalized and distinctive," Parker says. "The collaboration with our clients is the most enjoyable and rewarding aspect of our work."

Charming stonework and picturesque windows create a sophisticated Georgian façade. **STONE SOLID**

NATURAL WONDER — *A cottage-inspired homestead leads a harmonious existence with its natural surroundings.*

PARKER & ASSOCIATES ARCHITECTS

STRATEGIC LIGHTING AND TIMBER-BEAM ACCENTS ADD WARMTH TO TRADITIONAL ARCHITECTURE.

THE DARK, WOODEN CEILING AND FLOOR PLAY AGAINST LIGHT CABINETRY IN THE KITCHEN FOR AN ELEGANT CONTRAST.

PARKER & ASSOCIATES ARCHITECTS

RECYCLED STONE FROM AN 80-YEAR-OLD SCHOOL BUILDING ADDS CHARACTER TO THE FORMAL ENTRANCE.

In a bow to Norman-style architecture, this home's splendor lies in its simplicity and strength. **STATUESQUE STRENGTH**

BURDGE & ASSOCIATES

california

The work of Douglas Burdge, AIA, principal and founder of the architectural firm Burdge and Associates, and Jose Iujvidin, president, is trademarked as "Rustern." This melding of an informal rustic feel with a more modern interpretation of design has been described as transitional. Burdge's projects reveal a respect for the great architecture of the past coupled with design techniques appropriate for today's lifestyle. The firm believes its success is based on satisfying client desires and needs using the firm's exceptional design and well-thought-out planning. This service-based philosophy is accomplished by attentively listening to clients, commissioning for particular projects, and organizing rooms and areas into a workable plan that enhances the relationship between the homeowners and their living space. The projects also keep in mind possibilities to incorporate the use of green and sustainable design. "Great artistry is all about the best materials with the best proportions," says Douglas Burdge.

This family compound, with its open floor plan, is formal in appearance but easy to live in. **TUSCAN FEEL**

BIG WOOD RIVER *Every room of this 11,000-square-foot mountain home has maximized views of the river.*

BURDGE & ASSOCIATES

THIS CASUAL KITCHEN'S DESIGN TAKES ADVANTAGE OF THE EXPANSIVE, EXPOSED-BEAM CEILING.

BURDGE & ASSOCIATES

A VAULTED CEILING AND TEAK WOOD ACCENT THIS SPACIOUS LIVING AREA.

Mexican tile, stone fountains, Saltillo pavers and transom windows serve as warm finishes to this modern 5,200-square-foot casa.

HACIENDA HAVEN

LA COCINA | *Decorative niches, vibrant colors and ample windows increase the sense of warmth and enhance the play of light.*

BURDGE & ASSOCIATES

THIS HILLSIDE HOME CAPTURES VISTAS OF THE SURROUNDING AREA, WHILE ITS BARREL-TILE ROOF REFLECTS THE CALIFORNIA SUN.

ALLEN-GUERRA DESIGN-BUILD

breckenridge, colorado

When resources, materials and technologies converge to create an awe-inspiring home, the team at Allen-Guerra Design-Build has accomplished its goal. Erecting structures that are more than just the physical sums of their parts, the firm's passion is evident in the crisp, sophisticated lines of its creations and in the strides it takes to ensure that its clients will be completely satisfied with the end product. Allen-Guerra Design-Build has an uncanny understanding of the nuances of home building, instilling elements of its clients' personalities into the subtleties of the design, based upon an intimate knowledge of their habits, lifestyles, needs and desires. It is an intimacy that is fostered by the firm's commitment to establishing a relationship with each client, beyond mandatory design consultations. The result is a home that captures the essence of the individuals that inhabit it, while making a strong statement of aesthetic excellence on the landscape that it occupies.

This reinterpretation of a classic log cabin ignites a somber, nighttime sky with majestic lighting.

CABIN COUTURE

GRANDEUR KNOCKS *A regal entrance boasts extravagant wooden details and complex symmetry to awe and welcome visitors.*

ALLEN-GUERRA DESIGN-BUILD

WARM CEILING BEAMS AND A NATURAL STONE FIREPLACE DELIGHT WITH A CASUAL, COUNTRY FEEL.

ALLEN-GUERRA DESIGN-BUILD

HEAVY, WOODEN LOGS FRAME THE SITTING AREA AND CAPTURE ITS ROUGH, INFORMAL AMBIENCE.

A FARM-STYLE KITCHEN BORROWS INSPIRATION FROM CONTEMPORARY BUILDING ELEMENTS.

Rudimentary composition contributes to the traditional and dignified exterior of a modern log cabin.

LUXURY LOGGED

CHERI BELZ, ARCHITECT

boulder, colorado

Cheri Belz specializes in modern, organic-styled custom homes with an Asian flair. Each home, with a unique flow of forms and spaces, is approached with a deep respect for the environment, incorporating passive solar gain and using natural regional materials. Her designs are site specific, with the form and scale of the project carefully integrated into the landscape. Designing around existing elements rather than uprooting mature trees or natural boulders leads to a curious interplay between curves and linear planes that are then echoed in the roof forms. This has become one of the trademarks for which Belz is known and admired. Initially trained as a fine artist, she spent nearly a decade exhibiting in galleries and museums. This led to a deep appreciation for sculptural forms and the evolving aspect of architecture that is apparent in both her process and final designs. Projects begin with a basic design, which is enhanced by a collaborative effort of artists who work alongside Belz during construction in completing the details of each home. These include metal sculptors for stairways; woodworkers for cabinetry; concrete artists for cast tubs, sinks and countertops; door carvers; and landscape architects.

Nestled into the hillside, this home's "green" sod roof deck affords 360-degree views of the surrounding landscape.

GOING GREEN

NATURAL ELEMENTS *Existing boulders and trees were preserved by designing the house around and over them.*

CHERI BELZ, ARCHITECT

WALLS OF GLASS BRING THE OUTSIDE INTO THE KITCHEN.

THE CURVED STAIR WITH CUSTOM METAL RAILING FLOATS OVER THE FAMILY ROOM.

THIS LUXURIOUS MASTER BATH HAS A CAST-CONCRETE TUB AND GLASS-MOSAIC TILED STEAM SHOWER.

THIS CARVED MAHOGANY DOOR WITH INLAID STONE OPENS TO A SKYLIT FOYER WITH A NICHED, CURVED ART WALL.

CHERI BELZ, ARCHITECT

STAGGERED AND CANTILEVERED SPACES WITH ABUNDANT GLASS OFFER BREATHTAKING VIEWS.

WINDOWS IN THE TWO-LEVEL FOYER PROVIDE PASSIVE SOLAR GAIN.

Contrasting curvilinear and angular planes provide an interesting and inviting entry façade.

PLAY OF PLANES

AM JOHNSON ARCHITECTS

florida

Before founding his own architectural firm in Naples, A. Michael Johnson, AIA, was director of design for a large builder/developer company in Florida and partner in an architectural firm serving Florida and New Jersey. In both these firms, he gained valuable and practical experience in both architecture and construction. For the past ten years, his own firm, AM Johnson Architects, has been designing fine architectural projects, upscale single-family custom homes, multifamily custom residences, and a plethora of commercial projects in Southwest Florida, from Marco Island to Sanibel Island, along with residential projects in New Jersey. With a liking for traditional Mediterranean and Old Florida, Key West styling, Johnson's designs add modern flair while keeping the client's vision always at the forefront. By applying the architectural and design team's talents and attention to detail, a client's dream home soon becomes reality. The work of AM Johnson Architects not only wins accolades from satisfied clients and several awards in the field, but also results in word-of-mouth recommendations to friends, family and neighbors, and receives referrals from associates in the construction field.

A two-story, 5,000-square-foot Mediterranean house in The Brooks Country Club captures breathtaking views of the golf course. **MODERN MEDITERRANEAN**

AM JOHNSON ARCHITECTS

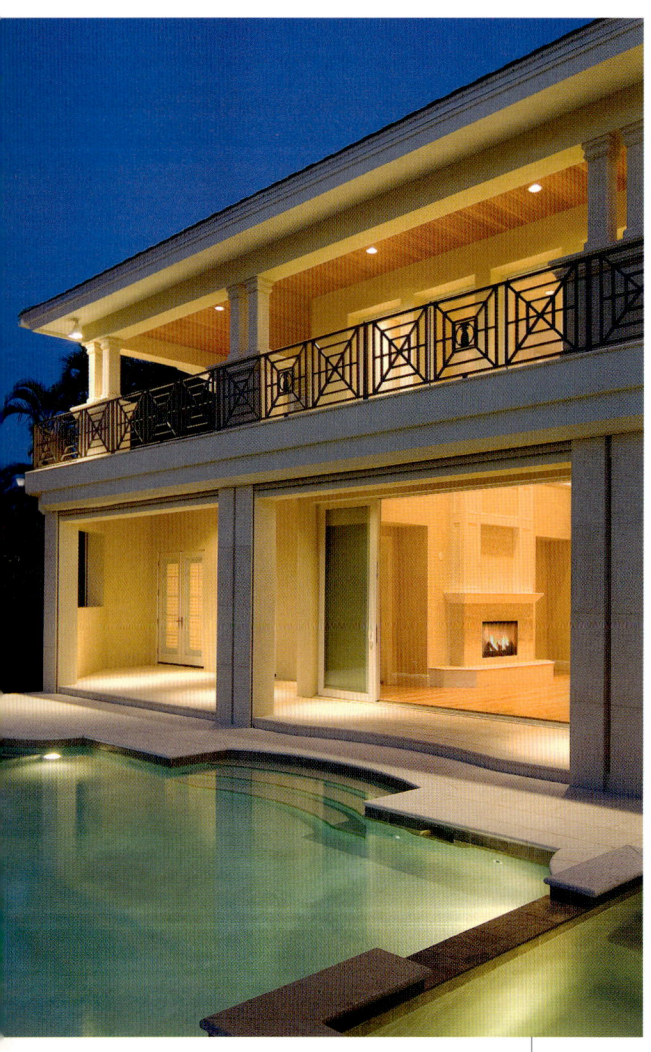

CYPRESS-PANELED CEILINGS GRACE THE LARGE, SWEEPING VERANDA OVERLOOKING THE POOL AND VENETIAN BAY.

THE MASTER BATH SHOWER'S EXPANSIVE WINDOWS TAKE ADVANTAGE OF THE PRIVATE COURTYARD.

Flanked by two two-car garages, the motor court introduces the concept of symmetry to this 6,000-square-foot Bermuda design.

SYMMETRICAL DESIGN

OUTDOOR LIVING — *The large outdoor living area, synonymous with the Florida lifestyle, includes a screened lanai, wet bar and outdoor kitchen.*

AM JOHNSON ARCHITECTS

THIS SCENIC MASTERPIECE INCORPORATES
HURRICANE-RESISTANT GLASS IN ITS DESIGN.

THE LEISURE ROOM'S POCKET SLIDING-GLASS WALLS DISAPPEAR
TO ALLOW A SEAMLESS TRANSITION FROM INDOORS TO OUTDOORS.

DECO DIVINE · *A tradition in Florida architecture, Deco embraces such features as curving lines and glass-brick details.*

AM JOHNSON ARCHITECTS

THIS KITCHEN BLENDS THE BEST OF DECO AND CONTEMPORARY STYLES.

DAWSON WISSMACH ARCHITECTS

georgia

Dawson Wissmach Architects' diverse team is passionate about contextual design, conservation of resources, working collaboratively and seeking out the specific characteristics each client brings to the process that will inform the direction of the design. Such characteristics include the history and traditions of the family, the vernacular language of the region and the special features of the site, as well as the inherent site constraints. The firm recognizes that the process of "defining home" is as one-of-a-kind as each unique client with whom they have the privilege of working. Rather than creating signature works, Dawson Wissmach Architects' goal at each project's end is the creation of a place that reflects the people who will call it home.

All rooms of this multi-structure home share a pristine view of the water. **REFINEMENT REFLECTED**

GUEST SERVICE *Guest quarters on the 29-acre compound overlook the May River.*

DAWSON WISSMACH ARCHITECTS

PINE FLOORING AND EXPOSED OAK BEAMS GIVE THIS STATE-OF-THE-ART KITCHEN A TRADITIONAL FEEL.

ORNATE OAK *A preserved 100-year-old live oak tree provides shade for the welcoming entry of a cottage home.*

DAWSON WISSMACH ARCHITECTS

A COASTAL RETREAT'S FORMAL ENTRY CATCHES VIEWS OF THE OUTDOORS.

DAWSON WISSMACH ARCHITECTS

THE CONNECTIVITY OF ONE AREA TO ANOTHER LENDS A FREE-FLOWING FEEL TO THE LIVING SPACE.

Three generations of family have admired the salt-water marshes from this 6,500-square-foot South Carolina vacation home.

FAMILY TRADITION

MCLAUGHLIN & ASSOCIATES ARCHITECTS

idaho

McLaughlin & Associates is a firm known for creating timeless designs that satisfy the functional and emotional needs of its clients. The firm's highly interactive and collaborative approach to design, and its devoted involvement in the building process and beyond, yields architectural and planning solutions that cater to each client's specific needs. Established in 1975, the full-service firm is renowned for its custom resort, residential and commercial designs, creating dramatic yet intimate interiors with the help of natural materials for a truly organic aesthetic. The firm prides itself on its ability to blur the distinction between interior and exterior, responding to a structure's surroundings and restoring harmony to the building and its environment. With impressive projects on display in several states and abroad, McLaughlin and Associates has garnered a host of national and international awards for both design and its work with natural materials.

Multiple peaked roofs provide charm and balance to the nature-inspired architecture.

LAKESIDE LUXURY

RUGGED REFINEMENT — *Intricate stonework reflects the rugged appeal of expansive mountain views.*

MCLAUGHLIN & ASSOCIATES ARCHITECTS

A BEAMED CEILING AND VAST WINDOWS ADD DRAMA TO THE DINING QUARTERS.

CONTEMPORARY FURNISHINGS AND ARTWORK FORM A STARK CONTRAST AGAINST THE TRADITIONAL STONE WALLS.

MCLAUGHLIN & ASSOCIATES ARCHITECTS

DAPPLED SHADOWS MIMIC THE CASUAL BEAUTY OF THE TRELLISED BALCONY.

The stone and distressed-wood accents give a cozy feel to the formal dining room.

WESTERN WARE

ISLAND TIME — *Lush landscaping and an inviting Jacuzzi transform this backyard into a tropical oasis.*

MCLAUGHLIN & ASSOCIATES ARCHITECTS

ROMANTIC WAVES ARE THE FOCAL POINT OF THIS BEACHSIDE BUNGALOW.

INTIMATE FURNISHING CLUSTERS BRING WARMTH TO THE LARGE, OPEN SPACE.

THE LYONS DESIGN GROUP

illinois

Personality and practicality define the work of The Lyons Design Group. The firm believes a residence should reflect the personality and needs of its owner, invoke comforting feelings for those using its spaces, and enhance the features of the surrounding environment. Adam Lyons' masterful ability to bring the clients' visions and desires into reality is achieved through a thorough investigation of conceptual solutions by implementing elements from an array of architectural styles, and by working hand-in-hand with clients. The designs of The Lyons Design Group are able to surpass the mere "built environment," as attention to every aspect of the home in detail and consideration to proper scale, proportion and harmony are well planned. The firm's efforts result in designs of everlasting beauty.

Repeated arch-top windows create soft lines and unity in a Lake Forest Estate home. **CATCHY CURVES**

THE LYONS DESIGN GROUP

NUMEROUS WINDOWS MAXIMIZE DRAMATIC VIEWS.

THE SYMMETRY OF THE ENTRY FOYER AND FAMILY SPACE ARE ENFORCED BY FLANKING COLUMNS AND COFFERED CEILINGS.

A PANORAMIC PERSPECTIVE IS ACHIEVED VIA FLOOR-TO-CEILING WINDOWS AND DOORS.

THE MASTER BATH SUITE IS SET BY AN INTERPLAY OF ARCHED ELEMENTS.

This multi-level brick and stone home takes advantage of the sloping elevation.

ELEVATION EASE

COLONIAL CONTEMPORARY — *The gambrel roofs and brick chimney lend a sense of colonial whimsey to this home.*

THE LYONS DESIGN GROUP

CONTRASTING COLORS ON THE STAIRCASE EMPHASIZE ITS GRACEFUL CURVES.

THE FORMALITY OF THE LIVING ROOM IS HEIGHTENED BY A CATHEDRAL CEILING.

THE WROUGHT-IRON CHANDELIER AND EXPOSED TRUSSES ADD TO THE CEILING'S SYMMETRY.

THIS SITTING AREA GAINS A SENSE OF INTIMACY FROM ITS FRENCH ENTRY DOORS, STONE FIREPLACE AND MATCHING WOOD TRIM.

WELLS + ASSOCIATES ARCHITECTS

iowa

With origins dating back to 1926, Wells + Associates is an Iowa-based architecture firm offering a complete range of services, from programming, feasibility studies and master planning through architectural, interior and sustainable design. Nationally recognized for distinctive solutions that meld technology and material with place and precedent, the firm engages in commissions that integrate the principles of sustainable design into a wide range of work that includes governmental, civic, educational, collegiate, long-term healthcare, religious, medical, housing, industrial and commercial projects. Long before "green" became part of the contemporary lexicon, the firm designed responsible buildings and systems that continue to serve as models of sustainable architecture. Wells + Associates values its clients as active collaborators in finding solutions consistent with their needs. The firm produces original, yet timeless buildings that express the people, purpose and place that they are intended to serve. During its long tenure, Wells + Associates has earned a reputation for innovation and commitment to durability, economic responsibility and timely service.

A birdwalk provides a parallel and unhindered view of the home, drawing the indoors out.

LOOKING IN

WELLS + ASSOCIATES ARCHITECTS

A STUDY IN GEOMETRIC ELEGANCE, THE CURVED COUNTERTOP REFLECTS THE CURVATURE OF THE HOME.

EASILY ACCESSIBLE LIVING SPACES MAKE A CONTEMPORARY AND INVITING STATEMENT.

A sleek water feature provides a modern element of refinement to the residence's rural charm.   WATER WORKS

LIVING COLOR | *A pop of color adds a stylish and dramatic flair to the clean lines of the great room.*

WELLS + ASSOCIATES ARCHITECTS

THE KITCHEN AND GREAT ROOM MAKE UP PART OF THE "LIVING ZONE." MATERIALS ARE WARM AND NATURAL, AND FLOW FROM OUTSIDE IN.

THE FRONT DOOR IS TUCKED NEATLY UNDER SOARING WOOD OVERHANGS, REINFORCING THE HOME'S MODEST AND UNASSUMING PLACE IN ITS NEIGHBORHOOD.

KEN TATE ARCHITECT

louisiana

Practicing from a turn-of-the-century mansion in Madisonville, Louisiana, Ken Tate Architect has a fitting base of operation. One of the leading names in the field of classical and traditional architecture, Ken Tate founded his firm in 1984 knowing there were aspects of traditional design that remained untouched. Through his large body of residential work, Tate has been able to illustrate that traditional architecture can have a voice with beauty and purpose in today's landscape. Ken Tate Architect has rapidly grown to become an important and highly regarded firm, winning numerous awards and being featured in various book and magazine editorials. Ken Tate Architect has intentionally managed to remain small and plans to continue to do so in order to maintain a hands-on approach for every project and accomplish a consistency in its design philosophy.

This rear view of a Normandy-style farmhouse on 2,000 acres showcases stone walls and an antique slate roof.

NORMANDY NUANCE

FRENCH FLAIR *The herb garden and front courtyard have views of the natural stucco turret, which houses the stairwell.*

KEN TATE ARCHITECT

THE FIREPLACE MANTEL IS HAND-CARVED STONE, CIRCA 1755, FROM FRANCE.

THE ANTIQUE HEART PINE BEAMS ACCENT THE CLAY FLOOR TILES AND KITCHEN ISLAND LEGS, WHICH ARE IMPORTED FROM FRANCE.

KEN TATE ARCHITECT

THIS 1930S-INSPIRED HALL HAS A PLASTER GROIN-VAULTED CEILING.

THE SEATING AREAS ON THE PORTICO AND TERRACE PROVIDE AMPLE RELAXING SPACE TO ENJOY THE REAR YARD.

The coffered-ceiling breakfast room has an open view of the dramatic staircase.

ON THE RISE

PALLADIAN INSPIRATION | *The simplicity of this Baton Rouge villa is enhanced by the Roman-style tile roof imported from Italy.*

KEN TATE ARCHITECT

THE GRAND SALON IS A PERFECT COMPLEMENT TO THE GRANDEUR OF THE FORMAL DINING ROOM.

JOHN MORRIS ARCHITECTS

maine

With a strong emphasis on natural surroundings and the preservation of the environment, John Morris Architects creates unique homes that are in perfect harmony with their respective habitats. Established in 1974, the firm's work has become increasingly focused on the green movement, setting high objectives for sustainability and eco-friendly design without compromising its signature style or structural integrity. Renowned for its reinterpretation of 20th-century Arts & Crafts-style cottages and its attentive approach, John Morris Architects is committed to decreasing the environmental impact of new construction while delivering high-quality residential projects that are rich with architectural detail. This commitment is evident in the steps the firm takes to ensure that the design process, from concept to reality, is a creative and fun experience. As a client option for seamless project delivery, Morris Construction Services, a sister construction management firm, rigorously estimates project costs throughout design and ensures expedient delivery.

A sprawling compound sits high atop an imposing ledge with sweeping views of Muscongus Bay.

COASTAL AESTHETIC

JOHN MORRIS ARCHITECTS

A SECLUDED RETREAT EVOKES A SENSE OF SERENITY WITH LUSH FOLIAGE AND AN OCEANFRONT VISTA.

A handsome Arts & Crafts-style cottage—once a meager Cape—blends seamlessly with its surroundings.

WOODED RETREAT

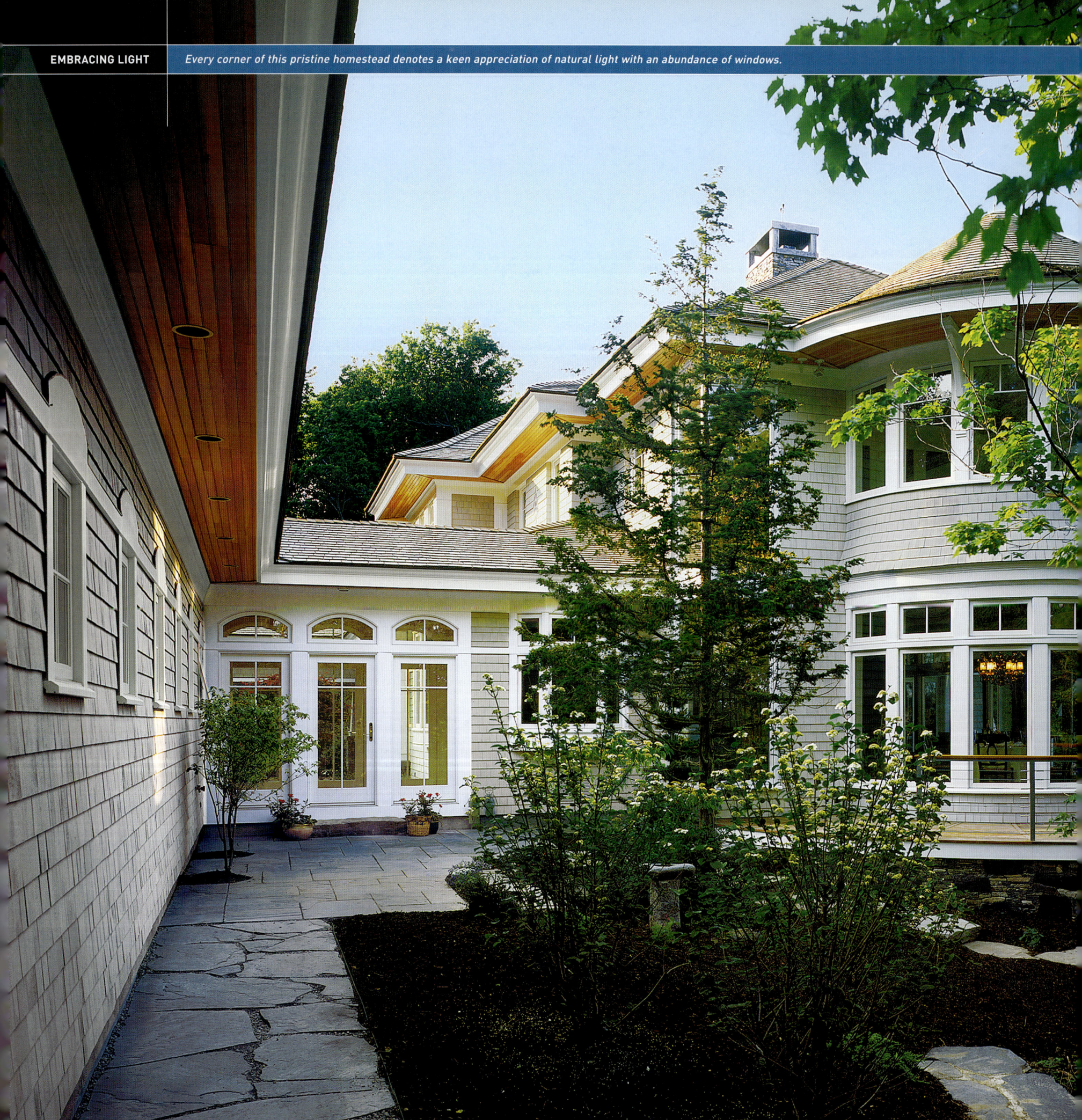

EMBRACING LIGHT *Every corner of this pristine homestead denotes a keen appreciation of natural light with an abundance of windows.*

JOHN MORRIS ARCHITECTS

THE CAREFULLY CONCEIVED FENESTRATION AND BALCONIES CULTIVATE
A RELATIONSHIP WITH THE OUTDOORS.

JOHN MORRIS ARCHITECTS

AN ELEVATED SCREENED PORCH PROVIDES PRIVACY WHILE CONTRIBUTING ARCHITECTURAL INTEREST.

A SECLUDED REAR DECK ENLISTS A CLASSIC PERGOLA TO FEND OFF THE SUN.

Small cottage charm abounds at this lakeside camp, featuring gabled bedrooms and carefully balanced windows for extensive water views.

COZY COTTAGE

LEVIN/BROWN & ASSOCIATES

maryland

Levin/Brown & Associates, Inc., is a multi-disciplined architectural firm located in Owings Mills, Maryland. The firm was founded in 1986 as a partnership between Jay Ira Brown, AIA, and Mark David Levin, AIA, and has concentrated its efforts on custom residential design since its inception. For Levin/Brown, each project starts with a discussion of what the client wishes to accomplish, to understand the goals and aspirations of each client. They are careful to ensure that every home responds to existing topography, existing and proposed vegetation, solar orientation and views, and accommodates the owner's interest in the development of outdoor living spaces. Each residence is a unique design, articulated to meet the functional, aesthetic and budgetary constraints of the owner. A unique distinction of the firm, Levin/Brown is capable of working in any architectural style. Levin/Brown welcomes the opportunity to work as a team with a client's interior designer, landscape architect and contractor in coordination with Levin/Brown's talented staff. The firm's clients speak highly of the creativity and flexibility of Levin/Brown, who are known as the "architects who listen."

The soft tones of the exterior stonework and steep, narrow roof lend poise and polish to a modern dwelling. AWED MUSING

STATELY SPLENDOR | *Sheer magnitude, regal columns and expansive windows establish the estate's imposing presence.*

LEVIN/BROWN & ASSOCIATES

A SPIRAL STAIRCASE DESCENDS WITH GLASS SIDES
TO TAKE ADVANTAGE OF THE VIEWS BELOW.

LEVIN/BROWN & ASSOCIATES

PARQUET FLOORS AND CLASSIC ACCENTS REFLECT OPULENT LEANINGS AND EXQUISITE TASTE.

A SHADED CHANDELIER AND A LENGTHY, ROBUST TABLE SET A FORMAL TONE IN THE DINING ROOM.

Picturesque peaks and worn, wooden detailing instill a country-style home with lighthearted panache. JOVIAL FLAIR

ROB BRAMHALL ARCHITECTS

massachusetts

Rob Bramhall Architects is a designer of fine custom homes, estates and vacation properties. These are most often in waterfront, woodland or mountain settings, but are also found in urban and ex-urban communities throughout the Northeast and eastern Canada. Established in 1991, the small, full-service architectural practice is best known for its design of townhouses, country houses, guesthouses, boathouses, barns, cottages and outbuildings. The firm's expertise is well-rounded, with a presence in the design of institutional, resort and recreational facilities and in select cluster communities. Offering more than thirty years of experience in both architecture and construction, Rob Bramhall's love of the West coupled with his New England roots have given form to an architectural style that encompasses history, tradition and a reverence for the land. The work further embraces a timelessness that results from delicately balancing form and proportion with quality materials, well-conceived details and well-crafted finishes.

Uniquely placed windows draw attention to the home's dramatic rooftops.

PERFECTLY PEAKED

PASTORAL PARCEL — *Detailed, New England forms and materials are a reflection of the surrounding landscape's unique character.*

ROB BRAMHALL ARCHITECTS

OVERSIZED WINDOWS AND DOORS ADMIT VIEWS OF LANDSCAPE AND LIGHT.

THIS BARREL-VAULTED CEILING AND GRACEFUL STAIRWAY LEND A DRAMATIC AND AIRY QUALITY TO THE FOYER.

ROB BRAMHALL ARCHITECTS

THE FRONT DRIVE MEANDERS THROUGH A LUSH COURTYARD.

Patio spaces, plantings and the natural use of woodlands contribute to a relaxed and informal outdoor space. **GREAT OUTDOORS**

DOMINICK TRINGALI ARCHITECTS

michigan

Dominick Tringali Architects is a classically based architecture firm with its main focus for all projects revolving around the three elements of good design: form, function and beauty. This trinity, combined with the firm's philosophy of "lifestyle by design," is the principle behind the firm's fast-growing success. Under Tringali's leadership, the firm has grown into a team of 25 talented individuals who all share a common passion for the firm's mission: "Live life, share dreams, experience design." Now registered in 11 states, DTA continues to expand into new regions of the country, bringing their award-winning designs into new markets. The firm's portfolio of custom homes, communities, multifamily developments and specialty commercial projects across the country capture the essence of DTA's distinguished design flavor, and are each created with the firm's core philosophy in mind—designing each project in conjunction with the client's lifestyle.

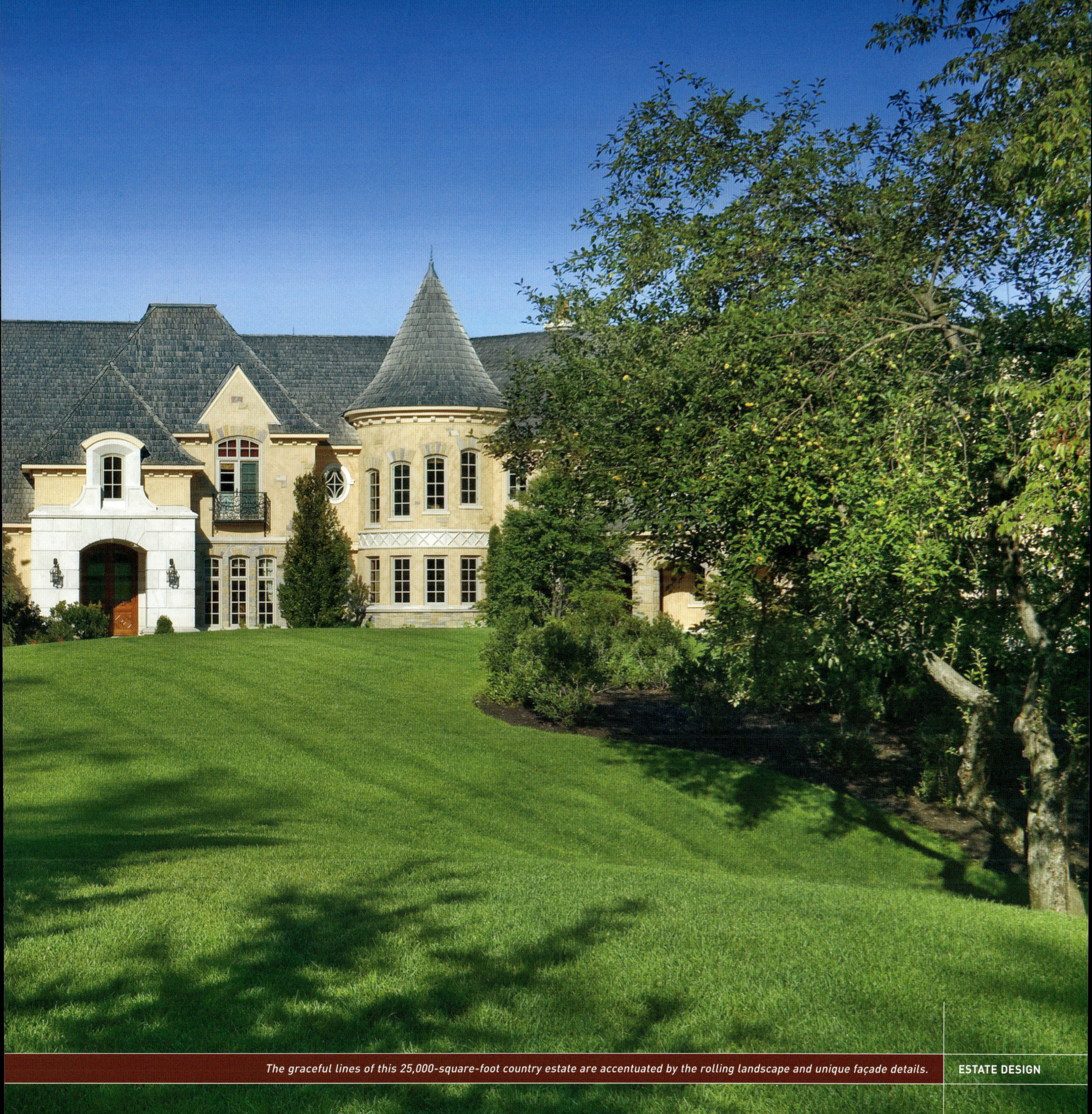

The graceful lines of this 25,000-square-foot country estate are accentuated by the rolling landscape and unique façade details. **ESTATE DESIGN**

TRADITIONAL LINES *This exterior living space was designed as a retreat in conjunction with the client's lifestyle.*

DOMINICK TRINGALI ARCHITECTS

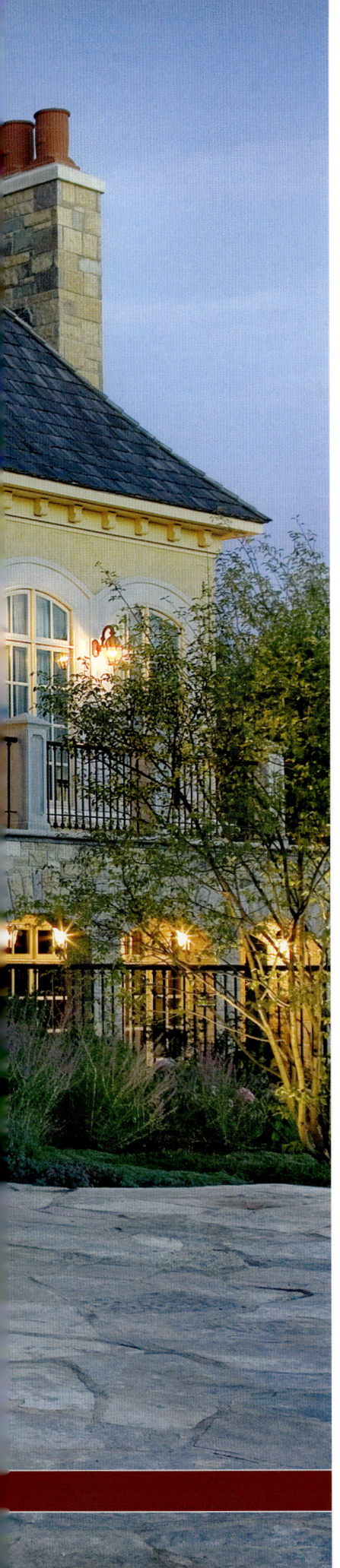

CLEAN LINES AND COMMERCIAL-GRADE BRICK CAPTURE THE HOME'S TRANSITIONAL FLAVOR.

DOMINICK TRINGALI ARCHITECTS

THE CONTEMPORARY MASTER BATHROOM OVERLOOKS THE SURROUNDING VISTAS.

LARGE PANES OF GLASS IN THE DINING ROOM LOOK OUT ON DRAMATIC SCENERY.

The pool and infinity-edge spa share interior views of the house through floor-to-ceiling windows.

WATER'S EDGE

CURVY COMPLEMENT *The dramatic curves and angles of the architecture are reflected in the garden.*

LIFESTYLE BY DESIGN IS HIGHLIGHTED BOTH INDOORS AND OUTDOORS.

BRIGGS ARCHITECTURE + DESIGN

montana

Briggs Architecture + Design creates homes, lodges and resort projects that are as individual and diverse as its clientele. Often, the firm is challenged to design unique details and accessories to complement existing architecture, bringing the spaces to life and defining the character of the home. Led by principal Donald G. Briggs, AIA, Briggs Architecture + Design believes that a successful project begins with the art of listening. This ensures that the home is a true reflection of the owner, not the architect. Briggs often tells his clients that he intends to design their home the way they would if they were architects themselves. The firm is committed to harmonizing a building with its natural environment. This ethic is motivated by a deep respect for nature and a desire to create homes with sustainable style. These homes are designed to make efficient and elegant use of indigenous resources and built with healthy materials to create an environment that nurtures the body, as well as the spirit. These timeless designs continue to bring comfort, security and serenity to their inhabitants as the years unfold.

A classically designed Missouri estate inspires awe with an abundance of locally quarried stone. **LOCAL FLAVOR**

CAPTIVATING STAIR *Extravagant stone steps, texturally bound to the magnificent stone exterior, lead from the back patios to lakeside relaxation.*

BRIGGS ARCHITECTURE + DESIGN

A BARREL-VAULTED CEILING AND EXQUISITE FIREPLACE DRESS THE SITTING ROOM IN FORMALITY.

FINELY CRAFTED MILLWORK, ORNATE MOLDINGS AND A GLAZED SKYLIGHT ENRICH AN OCTAGONAL OFFICE.

BRIGGS ARCHITECTURE + DESIGN

STONE AND TIMBER AMPLIFY THE OLD WORLD ALLURE OF THIS FRENCH COUNTRY COTTAGE.

Anchored in stone and timber, the heart of this mountain-style home is enlivened with abundant natural light.

BROUGHT TO LIGHT

AVANT ARCHITECTS

nebraska

Aesthetically pleasing interiors with features designed for function; architecturally ingenious exteriors that capture the artistic tradition of the construction process; a unity between the indoors and outdoors that showcases a close, fluid relationship. The images triggered by these descriptions are staples in Avant Architects' arsenal of quality, cutting-edge designs. Offering both architectural and interior design services, the firm works to articulate its clients' desires with warmth and clarity, plotting each space as a reflection of the intended user's image and seeking his or her input for a truly interactive experience. This process results in finished products that encourage homeowners to understand the space and appreciate its emotional undercurrents, while providing maximum utility and function. A rare mixture of beauty and purpose emerge from homes envisioned and implemented by the talented team at Avant Architects, resulting in award-winning structures and interior designs that stand alone as testaments to elegance and excellence.

Transparency allows the sophisticated styling of the indoor spaces to read as part of the exterior.

INSIDE OUT

BLANK SLATE *Natural daylight highlights the slate floors and limestone walls in a contemporary, formal dining area.*

AVANT ARCHITECTS

ORGANIC MATERIALS AND ABUNDANT LIGHTING ARE MAINSTAYS IN THIS COMFORTABLE, FAMILY GATHERING SPACE.

AVANT ARCHITECTS

AN OPEN, LOFT-LIKE CONFIGURATION GRANTS THIS KITCHEN UNCONVENTIONAL DISTINCTION.

A RAW, MODERN EDGE IS ESTABLISHED BY INDUSTRIAL COMPONENTS AND DIVERSE TEXTURES.

Strong, masculine forms and deliberate design nuances bring clarity to the façade of a modern homestead. NOUVEAU NUANCE

THOMAS BAIO ARCHITECT

new jersey

With a thorough grasp of architectural precedent, Thomas Baio Architect draws upon historical building forms and concepts, juxtaposing them with its clients' needs and dreams to produce fresh and inventive design solutions. Principal Thomas Baio's unique architectural perspective contributes to residential designs that are appropriate, affordable and one of a kind. "The world is an eclectic place," Baio says. "That idea is the basis for all of our work and the fulfillment of our clients' visions." But before that vision can be honored, the seasoned professionals at Thomas Baio Architect cultivate relationships with clients. "Open communication and discussion about what our clients do and don't want allow us to better accomplish the desired results," Baio adds. Welcoming client participation is a hallmark of the firm, allowing Baio to craft timeless design schemes that will transform homeowners' dreams into realities, without breaking their spirits or their budgets. And while there is a technical aspect to the firm's offerings, evaluating site conditions, materials and building technology, Baio remains committed to historically recognizable, refreshingly distinct architecture with modern vitality.

A melding of different building forms, this home spans generations of design with effortless poise. BLENDED GRACE

LIGHT SHOW — *A tribute to Americana, a daring venture into form and expression manifests itself as curbside appeal.*

THOMAS BAIO ARCHITECT

MASSIVE TIMBER TRUSSES BRING DRAMATIC HEIGHTS TO AN INVITING, COMFORTABLE GREAT ROOM.

THOMAS BAIO ARCHITECT

INTRICATE MILLWORK MOLDS A HOME OFFICE INTO A REFINED, PROFESSIONAL ENVIRONMENT.

THIS FAMILY-FRIENDLY KITCHEN BENEFITS FROM THE INTRIGUE OF DETAILS AND CRAFTSMANSHIP.

A finely crafted residence beckons with architectural integrity and compositional interest. **GREEN SCENE**

BOULER DESIGN GROUP

new york

Bouler Design Group is an architectural collaborative dedicated to designing buildings that are aesthetically, ecologically and conceptually progressive. Its designs are innovative in how they connect materials with location, developing spaces that are elegant, efficient and, foremost, livable. The firm is known for integrating new technology without sacrificing comfort, and for making abundant use of sustainable energy. Based in Long Island, New York, BDG chooses not to focus its designs on any particular style of architecture. Instead, architect James Bouler, architectural designer Nicholas Pfluger and the entire creative team are committed to reflecting the taste and vision of clients, respecting the surrounding vernacular and using materials that provide long-term beauty and performance.

The three-car garage and second-story living space are crowned with a steep-angled roof, complemented by the turret to its right.

PERFECTLY BALANCED

LONG ISLAND LIVING *The gently arched "eyebrow" roof over the patio, which continues into the home as the kitchen's ceiling, is a pleasant juxtaposition to the strongly angled peaks of the hom*

BOULER DESIGN GROUP

OPEN TO THE KITCHEN BELOW, THE CURVING STAIRCASE FURTHER REFLECTS THE HOME'S ATTENTION TO ELEGANT LINES.

REMSENBURG RENOVATION *The sweeping gambrel roof line is carried to all facets of the residence.*

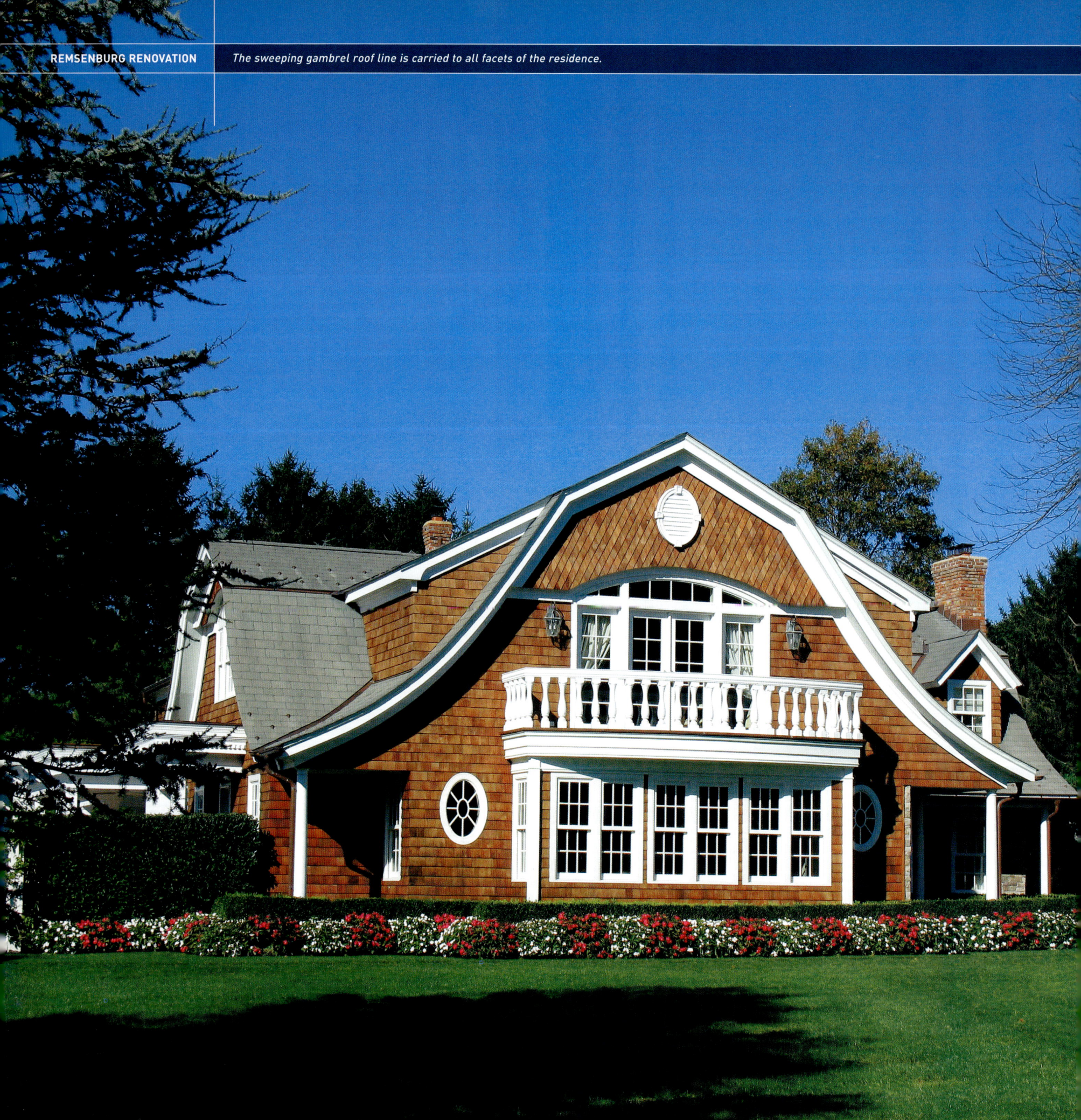

BOULER DESIGN GROUP

TRADITIONAL FARM-HOUSE LINES WERE INTRODUCED THROUGH THE RENOVATION.

SEASIDE HAVEN — *The home's balconies, positioned for privacy, share enhanced views of the bay.*

BOULER DESIGN GROUP

THE FRONT ELEVATION OF THE HOME IS REPLETE WITH WINDOWS TO ENJOY VIEWS OF THE SURROUNDING LANDSCAPE.

FROM THE GREAT ROOM, THE BEAUTY OF THE BAY IS FRAMED BY AN ARCHED WALL OF GLASS AND A CUSTOM WOOD ARCH BEAM.

SHAMBURGER DESIGN STUDIO

north carolina

Shamburger Design Studio is a Hendersonville, NC, architecture firm that offers comprehensive architectural services from a diverse team of professionals. SDS believes each project is a reflection of the client's individual personality, the local vernacular and virtuous use of materials, and always brings fresh energy and ideas to these projects. Shamburger Design Studio's goals are not only to deliver a proper solution for each project, but also to ensure we produce a building or group of buildings with a spirit that is of the site and the client. The firm specializes in resort developments, multi-family homes, custom homes and romantic, second-home getaways. Buildings influence how we work, live and play. They should provide comfort, give security and foster the ideas of renewal and conservation. Buildings should work within a practical response to reality and budget, but they should also transcend time and fixed styles. SDS's buildings are more than mere product; they are expressive structures that reflect these ideas.

A delightful cottage is nestled into its mountain setting and reaches out to take hold of nature. HARVEST HOUSE

COTTAGE CONTRAST — *A stone chimney runs the height of the room, visually uniting the first and second floors with texture.*

SHAMBURGER DESIGN STUDIO

VIBRANT RED BUNK BEDS AND WOOD PANELING EMBODY A CAMP AESTHETIC.

SHARP LINES AND ABUNDANT WINDOWS INFUSE THE ROOM WITH AIR AND LIGHT.

SHAMBURGER DESIGN STUDIO

RELAXATION IS PARAMOUNT IN THIS TRANQUIL BEDROOM ENVELOPED IN A SOFT, SOOTHING PALETTE.

DELICATE RAILINGS FORM CONTRAST TO THE NATURAL MATERIALS AND EARTHEN TONES OF THE FLOOR.

THE LIVING ROOM'S NEUTRAL HUES ALLOW LUSTROUS FABRICS AND RICH CARPETING TO TAKE CENTER STAGE.

A BROAD, NATURAL STONE WALKWAY ENCOURAGES LEISURELY STROLLS ALONG THE HOME'S EXTERIOR, WITH VIEWS OF THE MOUNTAINS AND LAKE BELOW.

Straddling the line between traditional and contemporary, this distinctive residence defies classification. **CRAFTSMAN ELEGANCE**

RUSTIC ROMANCE *Minimal furnishings of whimsical wicker reinforce the room's strong relationship with the outdoors.*

SHAMBURGER DESIGN STUDIO

THIS MOUNTAIN COTTAGE MERGES MODERN LUXURY AND HISTORIC CHARM, WITH THE USE OF NATURAL MATERIALS THROUGHOUT.

ROSE-COLORED STONE AND A SOPHISTICATED SILHOUETTE LEND ROMANTIC ALLURE TO A MOUNTAIN-TOP ABODE.

JEFFREY L. MILLER ARCHITECT

oregon

Since its inception in 1982, Jeffrey L. Miller Architect, PC, has completed over 400 projects. Yet, despite its established contributions to residential design, the firm still endeavors to maintain a personalized approach to architecture. Miller's goal is to custom tailor homes to suit the needs of individual clients, with architecture that not only complements the owners' lifestyles, but also fulfills their dreams of what a home can be. Clients are encouraged to participate in the vital elements of the decision-making process, whether it's selecting materials for finishes or working to tweak aspects of the sketches, resulting in homes that are as different in style as the personalities that inhabit them. And for Miller, achieving that variety is a coveted challenge and source of inspiration.

Inspired by Palladian principles, an elaborate estate basks in the glory of its own grandeur.

ELABORATE ESTATE

TACTILE TEXTILES | *Detailed stonework enlivens a residence with color and texture.*

JEFFREY L. MILLER ARCHITECT

AN ADAPTATION OF A SPANISH VILLA BLENDS TRADITIONAL ELEMENTS WITH CONTEMPORARY FLAIR.

JEFFREY L. MILLER ARCHITECT

A STUDY IN SYMMETRY ADDS PERSONALITY TO A DIGNIFIED MANOR.

A HIGH-TECH CONTEMPORARY STRUCTURE DISGUISES ITSELF AS AN ELEGANT AND SIMPLE FARMHOUSE.

THE RUGGED CHARACTER OF A MOUNTAINSIDE DWELLING IS REFLECTED IN ITS ROCKY TERRAIN.

TUCKED INTO A PATCH OF DENSE TREES, A MODERN LOG CABIN INTERPRETATION MELDS INTO ITS ENVIRONMENT.

A palette of natural materials imparts a calm and tranquil sensibility to a European country house. FIELD OF DREAMS

CHRISTOPHER ROSE ARCHITECTS

south carolina

It is not uncommon for an architectural firm to have a passion for and appreciation of the architectural history surrounding the sites it develops. But when the principal architect is a seventh-generation South Carolinian, the impact is spectacular. Christopher Rose Architects not only individualizes each design to its client but also to the property's characteristics, accounting for the prevailing breeze, solar orientation and prominent views. No two of the firm's projects are the same, as Rose does not subscribe to one particular architectural style, his design palette ranging from contemporary to traditional. The design philosophy of Christopher Rose Architects, as well as its construction methods and materials, marry tried-and-true lessons of history with state-of-the-art techniques. Rose is known for working closely with his clientele and with the site's environment to capture that special something so that the structure he designs for it could fit nowhere else.

An enchanting guest house and pool form the central focus of this island family compound. ISLAND OASIS

SOUTHERN CHARM *Wrap-around porches provide a gracious transition from inside to outside entertaining areas.*

CHRISTOPHER ROSE ARCHITECTS

A SEPARATE GUEST HOUSE CREATES A WARM WELCOME AND OFFERS PRIVACY.

CHRISTOPHER ROSE ARCHITECTS

THE OPEN COLONNADE CREATES A SEAMLESS TRANSITION FROM THE ENTRY ROTUNDA TO THE GREAT ROOM.

A WROUGHT-IRON STAIRCASE WINDS GRACEFULLY TO THE SECOND STORY.

Wide entry stairs, a curved front door and porch help make this home inviting.

WARM WELCOME

CHRISTOPHER ROSE ARCHITECTS

THE BARREL-VAULT CEILING FRAMES THE VIEW OF THE OCEAN.

Decks on each level extend three viewing experiences while providing shade and cover.

SOUTHERN RETREAT

LOONEY RICKS KISS ARCHITECTS

tennessee

Timeless architectural fundamentals balanced with quality of life for today's world are hallmarks of the Housing Studio of Looney Ricks Kiss Architects. The firm brings its expertise to architecture, interiors, planning and research in virtually every component of residential and community design. Each design maximizes the day-to-day experience of its user and creates a memorable sense of place that is respectful of its location and surroundings, be they urban or rural. The LRK team has proven success and skill in balancing the formula for quality, quantity and cost of a project, whether it's high-end luxury or more modest. The firm credits its substantial accomplishments to its exceptional awareness of the marketplace and the high level of communication it enjoys with its clients. Offices of Looney Ricks Kiss can be found in Tennessee, Florida, New Jersey, Texas, Louisiana and Colorado. Since its founding in 1983, the firm has completed hundreds of projects throughout the United States, the majority of which are in the South and East. Projects have won wide recognition in various publications and numerous national and regional awards for design excellence. Carson Looney, FAIA, was inducted into the 2007 Wm. S. Marvin Hall of Fame for Design Excellence.

A dignified estate is defined by expressive stone construction that instills the home with soul.

SOULFUL SELECTION

GUIDING LIGHT *Each tier of this tri-level residence relies on windows and creative lighting to capture a lighthearted essence.*

LOONEY RICKS KISS ARCHITECTS

RELAXATION REACHES ITS PINNACLE IN A CLEAN,
ORGANIC BATHROOM WITH SLEEK LINES.

MINIMAL FURNISHINGS PAIRED WITH EXPANSIVE WINDOWS
INVITE VIEWS OF DISTANT HORIZONS.

LOONEY RICKS KISS ARCHITECTS

AN APPEALING OUTDOOR AREA LENDS INFORMAL CHARM TO A TRADITIONAL SHELTER.

A classic Colonial benefits from its sophisticated symmetry, finding renewed intrigue in conventional design. **REVIVED REFINEMENT**

VANGUARD STUDIO

texas

With a gift for innovative and artistic design, Vanguard Studio has successfully designed hundreds of projects since its creation in 2000, each highlighting the firm's passion for extraordinary architecture. Borrowing inspiration from the elegant contours and lines of Italian and Spanish structures of years past, Vanguard Studio combines timeless design traditions with contemporary and progressive ideals. The result is award-winning homes that are warm and casual in nature but maintain an aesthetic refinement that caters to the residents that inhabit them. Creating homes that ensure a client's vision is fully realized is the driving force for the firm's principal architect, John Hathaway. "We believe strong design that is responsive to the client's needs and dreams is always possible," he says, "no matter what constraints exist." With an experienced team, cutting-edge technology and professional integrity, Vanguard Studio provides clients with a broad range of options and ideas to suit every taste.

A contemporary hacienda combines the best of Spanish elegance with a refreshing, crisp outline.

HISTORICAL CHARM

DETAIL ORIENTED *Minute details pop against a heavily textured exterior, in contrast with the sleek water feature.*

VANGUARD STUDIO

RESTING IN THE DAPPLED SHADE, AN UNASSUMING ENTRANCE BOASTS SUBTLE ORNAMENTATION.

ELABORATE STONE ARCHWAYS DIFFUSE AND REFLECT LIGHT ONTO GLOSSY, WOODEN FLOORS.

LEADING RESIDENTIAL ARCHITECTS | 193

VANGUARD STUDIO

DELICATE CURVATURE, STATELY COLUMNS AND ORNATE RAILINGS DISTINGUISH A PALATIAL ABODE.

Neoclassical design is at its best in this dome-topped testament to detailed aesthetic excellence.   **DISTINGUISHED DOME**

ECLECTIC ARRANGEMENT | *Mosaic-like stonework converts traditional materials into an eclectic façade for this modern residence.*

VANGUARD STUDIO

WIDE ARCHWAYS DIVIDE A LARGE, AIRY SPACE INTO INDIVIDUAL ROOMS, ADDING A SENSE OF SCALE.

THIS OUTDOOR COURTYARD BOASTS ALL THE SOPHISTICATED SPLENDOR OF AN INDOOR ROOM.

JAFFA GROUP

utah

While the Jaffa Group's guiding principle is to maintain a strong commitment to design excellence, the firm also has a more practical tenet: Make the home-building experience an enjoyable one for everyone involved. With over 68 years of combined experience in the industry, father-son duo, Richard and Scott Jaffa, founded the firm in 1994 to pursue their shared architectural ideal of building homes with integrity, vision and distinction. What resulted was a thriving, homegrown enterprise that remains devoted to top-quality, superior service, while remaining sensitive to the needs of clients and their respective ideas, budgets and schedules. Whether it's a custom home, townhouse or a remodeling project, from conception to completion, the Jaffa Group strives to remain true to its mantras. While remaining uncompromising to its aesthetic morals, the firm designs each residence in accordance with the beauty of its natural landscape, ensuring unsurpassed customer satisfaction.

The sprawling roof's multiple points and peaks echo the ridges of a vast mountain backdrop.

OPULENT ODE

VANTAGE POINT — *Rows of glass and a curved, covered deck ignite allure in the backyard while providing unobstructed, scenic views.*

JAFFA GROUP

A PRISTINE LIVING AREA IS DEFINED BY CUSTOM IRONWORK AND DISTRESSED WALNUT FLOORS.

A COPPER COFFERED CEILING EXUDES AN AIR OF DECADENCE IN THE FORMAL DINING AREA.

JAFFA GROUP

TEN-FOOT DOORS AND STRATEGIC LIGHTING
FRAME AN IMPOSING ENTRANCE.

NATURAL MATERIALS, LIKE GRANITE AND RECLAIMED BARN WOOD,
MAKE A STRONG STATEMENT IN A MODERN KITCHEN.

A Park City home benefits from the liberal use of wooden accents and labored stone columns.

EMBRACING NATURE

SUMMER SLOPES — *With no snow on the slopes, a Deer Valley retreat becomes its own attraction with superior architectural details.*

JAFFA GROUP

POLISHED SINKS ACT AS POSH ACCENTS AGAINST THE NEUTRAL TONES OF WOOD AND GRANITE.

LIGHT COUNTERTOPS WITH FLECKS OF RICHER COLOR COMPLEMENT THE DARK, WALNUT CABINETRY AND DISTRESSED COPPER CEILING.

AN OPULENT APPRECIATION OF COLOR AND TEXTURE INFUSES THE HOME WITH RUSTIC ELEGANCE.

IN THE BATHROOM, HAND-CAST GLASS TILES AND ONYX COUNTERS IMPART AN ORGANIC FEEL.

J. GRAHAM GOLDSMITH ARCHITECTS

vermont

Appreciation for design and building began at age 10 for J. Graham Goldsmith as he used found materials to build elaborate tree houses. He then interned with a carpenter, an electrician, a mason and a plumber, which helped him understand design and construction. He was in Professor Louis Kahn's studio at the University of Pennsylvania, which taught him some of the most important architectural principles about daylight, spatial economy, and the appropriate use of materials. Those simple design elements now permeate the mood, character and atmosphere in his designs. Goldsmith's office in Burlington designs large-scale commercial and residential projects, while the Nantucket office focuses on custom high-end homes. His experience in both locations, where dramatic and sensitive environmental sites are more the norm, plays a significant role in his work, as well as sensitivity to the historical roots of surrounding architecture. He strives to create designs that carefully define goals based on the client's lifestyle and desires, and to creatively exceed expectations that harmonize light, space and materials with the surrounding environment.

A rambling summer home on Nantucket enjoys views of the harbor and conservation land from every vantage point.

REMINISCENT OF DAYS PAST

ANGLO CARIBBEAN — *A mix of older southern climate styles, this Florida home is inspired by historic Caribbean details.*

J. GRAHAM GOLDSMITH ARCHITECTS

A HARBOR-FRONT RESIDENCE ON NANTUCKET ISLAND.

STYLED AFTER THE MAIN HOUSE, THE POOL HOUSE AND OFFICE ALSO ENJOY BREATHTAKING VIEWS OF THE OCEAN.

J. GRAHAM GOLDSMITH ARCHITECTS

A WARM FOYER BOASTS CUSTOM MAHOGANY ENTRY DOORS.

THE CLASSIC SUMMERTIME LIVING ROOM LETS THE OUTDOORS IN.

THE MASTER BEDROOM SUITE HAS LIGHT-FILLED VIEWS FROM EVERY WINDOW.

FRENCH DOORS OPEN TO AN INTIMATE SECOND-STORY DECK.

Traditional detailing captures the simple, cottage ambience of this Nantucket Harbor-view home.

SEASIDE SANCTUARY

ARCHITECTONICS

washington

While structural soundness and integrity, as well as aesthetic allure, serve as the cornerstones in the design process employed by Architectonics, the company's vision extends far beyond the physical plane. The firm conducts business under the principles of quantum architecture, embracing the science of architecture, as well as the spirit of place. With over 32 years of experience in the industry, founder Moe Pezeshk constantly challenges the traditional confines of what makes a house a home, and his dedication is reflected in Architectonics' beautiful, healthy habitats that enhance clients' well-being through the management of energy flow within a structure. The award-winning firm's talented team of design professionals tirelessly envisions ways to instill each home with a sense of joy and tranquility. With careful attention to detail and mystifying manipulation of light and color, Architectonics brings to its designs an advanced appreciation of form and function, producing dwellings that are both harmonious with its clients' lifestyles and environment, and that possess the kind of timeless beauty that is continually evolving.

Crisp, geometric lines define this home with a strong character intensified by its simplicity of form. PURE FORM

CAPTIVATING FORCE *Suitable for a modern-day celebration, an interpretation of an Italian villa enlivens the landscape with bold color.*

ARCHITECTONICS

A GRAND PERGOLA WITH REGAL ROMAN ARCHES OVERLOOKS LAKE WASHINGTON.

ARCHITECTONICS

OPULENT RAYS OF SUN REFLECT ON THE CALM WATERS
OF THE POOL, MAKING IT A PEACEFUL RETREAT.

An ornate iron gate lends an exclusive air to the entrance of a sophisticated, stylish dwelling.

LUXURY'S CALL

CROWNING GLORY *careful fenestration ensures that light and outdoor views are abundant.*

ARCHITECTONICS

TWO STORIES OF ELABORATE COLUMNS DOMINATE THE DESIGN WITH TRADITIONAL YET VIVID DETAIL.

DUBBE-MOULDER ARCHITECTS

wyoming

Since its founding in 1996, Dubbe-Moulder Architects has offered services in residential, commercial and interior design, as well as in land planning and historic preservation. The firm is known for its quality design within a western environment and is particularly attentive to historical context, natural features and indigenous materials. Through a respect for the integrity and character of a region and site, the designers are able to unify structure and location to create beautiful and timeless compositions that connect people to place. Drawing inspiration from the Rocky Mountain-region landscape, Dubbe-Moulder Architects is dedicated to achieving the client's goal while taking the client's lifestyle into account. Each DMA project is executed with the understanding that refined architecture has always been complemented by excellent craftsmanship.

Like the water it is perched near, the home is set aglow by the evening sun reflecting upon its wood exterior. WARM GLOW

MAKE THE GRADE *The home takes advantage of the unique sloping grade of the property, as it seems to amble down the hill.*

DUBBE-MOULDER ARCHITECTS

THE USE OF SEVERAL SMALL WINDOWS CLUSTERED GEOMETRICALLY ACCENTUATES THE DRAMATIC ANGLE OF THE ROOF.

THE FLOOR-TO-CEILING WINDOWS BRING THE PINE FOREST INDOORS.

DUBBE-MOULDER ARCHITECTS

EACH PIECE OF WINTER-DAMAGED LODGEPOLE PINE WAS HAND SELECTED TO CREATE THE DESIRED LOOK.

This room's rustic contemporary theme is prevalent throughout the design of the home.

COWBOY CONTEMPORARY

ALL-SEASON RETREAT *An exterior fireplace lends architectural interest and warmth to an elevated patio, bringing living room comfort outdoors.*

DUBBE-MOULDER ARCHITECTS

STONE AND WOOD MATERIALS IN THE KITCHEN AND BREAKFAST AREA ARE REFLECTIVE OF THE OUTDOORS.

RAW TIMBER, SOFT LIGHTING AND BRICK CHIMNEYS ADD A FANCIFUL TOUCH TO THE HOME'S FAÇADE.

INDEX

A

ALLEN-GUERRA DESIGN-BUILD, INC.
1915 Airport Road, Suite 105
Breckenridge, CO 80424
Ph: 970-453-7002 ■ Fax: 970-453-7040
E-mail: info@allen-guerra.com
Web site: www.allen-guerra.com

AM JOHNSON ARCHITECTS
A. Michael Johnson, AIA
1205 Piper Boulevard, Suite 202
Naples, FL 34110
Ph: 239-597-7278 ■ Fax: 239-597-7305
E-mail: johnsonarchitects@gmail.com
Web site: www.amjohnsonarchitects.com

ARCHITECTONICS
1014 Market Street
Kirkland, WA 98033
Ph: 425-828-0329 ■ Fax: 425-889-8338
E-mail: MoeP@Architectonics-Inc.com
Web site: www.architectonics-inc.com

AVANT ARCHITECTS
3337 North 107th Street
Omaha, NE 68134
Ph: 402-493-9611 ■ Fax: 402-493-9629
E-mail: lkrejci@avant-architects.com
Web site: www.avant-architects.com

B

BLUE SKY STUDIO
6771 Lauden Circle
Anchorage, AK 99502
Ph: 907-677-9078 ■ Fax: 907-677-9079
E-mail: catherine@callbluesky.com
Web site: www.callbluesky.com

BOULER DESIGN GROUP
12 Doxsee Place
Islip, NY 11751
Ph: 631-969-3335 ■ Fax: 631-969-3391
E-mail: boulerdesign@optonline.net
Web site: www.boulerdesigngroup.com

BRIGGS ARCHITECTURE + DESIGN
120 South 5th Street, Suite 101
Hamilton, MT 59840
Ph: 406-375-1111 ■ Fax: 406-363-1414
E-mail: don@briggsarch.com
Web site: www.briggsarch.com

BURDGE & ASSOCIATES, ARCHITECTS, INC.
21235 Pacific Coast Highway
Malibu, CA 90265
Ph: 310-456-5905 ■ Fax: 310-456-2467
E-mail: doug@buaia.com
Web site: www.buaia.com

C

CHERI BELZ, ARCHITECT
601 Kalmia Avenue
Boulder, CO 80304
Ph: 303-995-6111 ■ Fax: 303-541-1011
E-mail: cheri@belzarch.com
Web site: www.belzarch.com

CHRISTOPHER ROSE ARCHITECTS, P.A.
3509 Meeks Farm Road
Johns Island, SC 29455
Ph: 843-559-7670 ■ 877-559-7670
Fax: 843-559-7673
E-mail: crose@chrisrosearchitects.com
Web site: www.christopherrosearchitects.com

D

DAWSON WISSMACH ARCHITECTS
12 East Bay Street
Savannah, GA 31401
Ph: 912-201-0111 ■ Fax: 912-201-0143
E-mail: rwissmach@dwarch.com
Web site: www.dwarch.com

DOMINICK TRINGALI ARCHITECTS, INC.
1668 Telegraph Road, Suite 250
Bloomfield Hills, MI 48302
Ph: 248-335-8888 ■ Fax: 248-335-0944
E-mail: JamieQ@DTArchitects.com
Web site: www.DTArchitects.com

DUBBE-MOULDER ARCHITECTS
P.O. Box 9227
1160 Alpine Lane, Suite 2A
Jackson Hole, WY 83002
Ph: 307-733-9551 ■ Fax: 307-733-4302
E-mail: dubbemoulder@dubbe-moulder.com
Web site: www.dubbe-moulder.com

H

HARRIS & ASSOCIATES, ARCHITECTS/PLANNERS LLC
3037 Massey Road
Birmingham, AL 35216-3603
Ph: 205-823-4884 ■ Fax: 205-978-8781
E-mail: rharris@harrisaa.com
Web site: www.harrisaa.com

J

J. GRAHAM GOLDSMITH, ARCHITECTS, P.C.
7 Kilburn Street
Burlington, VT 05401
Ph: 802-862-4053 ■ Fax: 802-864-8267
E-mail: vt@jggarchitects.com
Web site: www.jggarchitects.com

INDEX

JAFFA GROUP
1960 Sidewinder Drive, Suite 101
Park City, UT 84060
Ph: 435-615-6873 ■ Fax: 435-615-6917
E-mail: scott@jaffagroup.com
Web site: www.jaffagroup.com

JEFFREY L. MILLER ARCHITECT, P.C.
834 SW St. Clair Avenue #202
Portland, OR 97205-1322
Ph: 503-222-2234 ■ Fax: 503-222-6134
E-mail: jeff@jlmarchitect.com
Web site: www.jlmarchitect.com

JOHN MORRIS ARCHITECTS
49 Mechanic Street
Camden, ME 04843
Ph: 207-236-8321 ■ Fax: 207-236-6391
E-mail: info@johnmorrisarchitects.com
Web site: www.johnmorrisarchitects.com

K

KEN TATE ARCHITECT
P.O. Box 550
206 Covington Street
Madisonville, LA 70447
Ph: 985-845-8181 ■ Fax: 985-845-8182
E-mail: tate@kentatearchitect.com
Web site: www.kentatearchitect.com

L

LEVIN/BROWN & ASSOCIATES, INC.
15 Greenspring Valley Road
Owings Mills, MD 21117
Ph: 410-581-0104 ■ Fax: 410-581-0108
E-mail: jayb@levinbrown.com
Web site: www.levinbrown.com

LOONEY RICKS KISS ARCHITECTS, INC.
175 Toyota Plaza, Suite 600
Memphis, TN 38103
Ph: 901-521-1440 ■ Fax: 901-525-2760
E-mail: dlovett@lrk.com
Web site: www.lrk.com

M

MCLAUGHLIN & ASSOCIATES ARCHITECTS
126 Saddle Road
Ketchum, ID 83340
Ph: 208-726-9392 ■ Fax: 208-726-9423
E-mail: jim@mclaughlinarchitects.com
Web site: www.mclaughlinarchitects.com

P

PARKER & ASSOCIATES ARCHITECTS
100 West Center Street, Suite 103
Fayetteville, AR 72701-6063
Ph: 479-443-2030 ■ Fax: 479-443-1545
E-mail: terry@tparkerarch.com
Web site: www.tparkerarch.com

R

ROB BRAMHALL ARCHITECTS
14 Park Street
Andover, MA 01810
Ph: 978-749-3663 ■ Fax: 978-749-9659
E-mail: betsie@robbramhallarchitects.com
Web site: www.robbramhallarchitects.com

ROBINETTE ARCHITECTS, INC.
1670 East River Road, Suite 112
Tucson, AZ 85718
Ph: 520-323-3979 ■ Fax: 520-888-5518
E-mail: contact@robinettearchitect.com
Web site: www.robinettearchitect.com

S

SHAMBURGER DESIGN STUDIO
421 5th Avenue West
Hendersonville, NC 28739
Ph: 828-692-2737 ■ Fax: 828-694-0737
E-mail: designstudio@sdsaia.com
Web site: www.shamburgerdesignstudio.com

T

THE LYONS DESIGN GROUP, INC.
211 East Church Street
Libertyville, IL 60048
Ph: 828-692-2737 ■ Fax: 828-694-0737
E-mail: lyonsdesigngroup@aol.com
Web site: www.lyonsdesigngroupinc.com

THOMAS BAIO ARCHITECT
Principal Architect
Thomas Baio Architect PC
505 Main Street
Metuchen, NJ 08840
Ph: 732-603-2415 ■ Fax: 732-603-2418
Web site: www.ThomasBaioArchitect.com

V

VANGUARD STUDIO, INC.
6601 Vaught Ranch Road, Suite G-10
Austin, TX 78730
Ph: 512-918-8312 ■ Fax: 512-918-8313
E-mail: john@vanguardstudio.com
Web site: www.vanguardstudio.com

W

WELLS + ASSOCIATES ARCHITECTS
1105 Grand Avenue, Suite 200
West Des Moines, IA 50265
Ph: 515-327-0007 ■ Fax: 515-327-0077
E-mail: dwells@wells-plus.com
Web site: www.wells-plus.com

PHOTO CREDITS

Page 2-3: Architect: Dawson Wissmach Architects; Photography: Attic Fire Architectural Photography **Page 5:** Architect: Vanguard Studio; Photography: Coles Hairston **Page 6:** Architect: Robinette Architects; Photography: Jon Mancuso **Page 9:** Architect: Christopher Rose Architects; Photography: Rion Rizzo, Creative Sources Photography, Inc. **Page 10:** Architect: Levin/Brown & Associates; Photography: Alan Gilbert **Page 13:** Architect: Levin/Brown & Associates; Photography: Alan Gilbert **Page 14:** Architect: Levin/Brown & Associates; Photography: Alan Gilbert **Page 16-23:** Charles Beck Studios **Page 24-29:** Kevin G. Smith Photography **Page 30-33:** John Mancuso **Page 34-35:** Pam Singleton **Page 36:** Jon Mancuso **Page 37:** (LEFT) Jon Mancuso (RIGHT) Pam Singleton **Page 38-41:** De Shield-Marley, Shields-Marley Photography **Page 42-43:** James Keltner, Keltner & Associates **Page 44-45:** Mark Lohman **Page 46-47:** Kevin Syms **Page 48-49:** Distinctive Homes **Pages 50-51:** Mark Lohman **Page 52-55:** Monika Hilleary, Light Dance Studio **Page 56-57:** Living Images Photography **Pages 58-61:** Monika Hilleary, Light Dance Studio **Page 62-63:** Bryce Boyer **Pages 64-71:** Amber Fredriksen Photography **Pages 72-79:** Attic Fire Architectural Photography **Page 80-83:** Roger Wade **Pages 84-85:** (LEFT) Mary Nichols (RIGHT) Roger Wade **Pages 86-87:** Roger Wade **Page 88-93:** Ken Ferdman **Pages 94-98:** Timothy Hursley **Page 99:** (LEFT) Jamie Malloy (RIGHT) Timothy Hursley **Page 100-102:** Timothy Dunford **Pages 103:** (LEFT) Dan Bibbs (RIGHT) Timothy Dunford **Pages 104-105:** Timothy Dunford **Page 106-107:** (LEFT) Gordon Beall (RIGHT) Mara Cooper **Pages 108-109:** Brian Vanden Brink **Page 110-111:** Rob Karosis Photography **Page 112-113:** Westphalen Photography **Page 114-115:** Rob Karosis Photography **Pages 116-121:** Alan Gilbert **Page 122-127:** Alex Vertikoff, Martin and Reilly **Pages 128-129:** George Dzahritsos **Pages 130-131:** (LEFT) George Dzahritsos (RIGHT) Beth Singer Photographer, Inc. **Page 132-135:** James Haefner Photography **Pages 136-139:** Jeff Sweet **Pages 140-141:** (LEFT) Briggs Architecture + Design (RIGHT) Timothy Ludwig **Pages 142-147:** Tom Kessler **Pages 148-153:** Thomas Baio **Pages 154-161:** Jennifer Pfluger **Pages 162-169:** Matt Silk Photography **Page 170-171:** Robert Reynolds, Reynolds Wulf Design **Page 172-173:** (LEFT) Sally Painter Photography (RIGHT) Photography by Robert Reynolds, Reynolds Wulf Design **Page 174:** (UPPER LEFT) Sally Painter Photography; (UPPER RIGHT) Robert Reynolds, Reynolds Wulf Design (LOWER LEFT) Sally Painter Photography (LOWER RIGHT) Photography by Indivar Sivanathan **Pages 175:** Sally Painter Photography **Page 176-177:** Eric Prine; Attic Fire Architectural Photography **Page 178-183:** Rion Rizzo; Creative Sources Photography, Inc. **Pages 184-185:** Looney Ricks Kiss Architects, Inc. **Pages 186-187:** Jack Gardner Photography **Page 188-189:** Looney Ricks Kiss Architects, Inc. **Page 190-193:** Coles Hairston **Page 194-195:** Thomas McConnell **Page 196-197:** Coles Hairston **Page 198-204:** Richard Springate **Page 205:** Scott Zimmerman **Page 206-211:** Susan Teare **Page 212-219:** John G. Wilbanks Photography, Inc. **Page 220-221:** (LEFT) Carrie Patterson (RIGHT) Cameron Neilson **Page 222-226:** Cameron Neilson **Page 227:** (TOP) Cameron Neilson (BOTTOM) David J. Swift **Page 230:** Architect: McLaughlin & Associates Architects; Photography: Roger Wade **Page 233:** Architect: Dawson Wissmach Architects; Photography: Attic Fire Architectural Photography **Page 234-235:** Architect: John Morris Architects; Photography: Brian Vanden Brink **Page 236:** Architect: Christopher Rose Architects; Photography: Rion Rizzo, Creative Sources Photography, Inc. **Front Cover:** Christopher Rose Architects; Photography: Eric Prine, Attic Fire Architectural Photography **Back Cover:** (UPPER LEFT) Architect: Jaffa Group; Photography: Richard Springate (LOWER LEFT) Architect: Looney Ricks Kiss Architects; Photography: Terry Sweeney, Sweeney South Commercial Photography (UPPER RIGHT) Architect: AM Johnson Architects; Photography: Amber Fredriksen Photography (LOWER RIGHT) Architect: Cheri Belz, Architect; Photography: Bryce Boyer

Additional Credits: Page 116-121: Landscape: Bob Jackson of Bob Jackson Landscapes, Inc.; Interior Design: Jay Jenkins of Jenkins Baer Associates, Inc.